The Wild Life of
BIG CATS

By Camilla de la Bédoyère

WINDMILL
BOOKS

THE WILD SIDE

Published in 2015 by **WINDMILL BOOKS**, an Imprint of Rosen Publishing
29 East 21st Street, New York, NY 10010

Publishing Director: Belinda Gallagher
Creative Director: Jo Cowan
Editorial Director: Rosie Neave
Assistant Editor: Amy Johnson
Designers: Jo Cowan, Venita Kidwai
Image Manager: Liberty Newton
Production Manager: Elizabeth Collins
Reprographics: Stephan Davis, Jennifer Cozens, Thom Allaway, Lorraine King, Anthony Cambray

ACKNOWLEDGEMENTS

The publishers would like to thank Mike Foster (Maltings Partnership), Joe Jones, and Richard Watson (Bright Agency) for
the illustrations they contributed to this book. All other artwork from the Miles Kelly Artwork Bank.

The publishers would like to thank the following sources for the use of their photographs: t = top, b = bottom, l = left,
r = right, c = center, bg = background, rt = repeated throughout. **Cover** (front) Sergey Gorshkov/Minden Pictures/FLPA;
(back) Stuart G Porter/Shutterstock; (Joke panel) Tropinina Olga. **Corbis** 21(b) Andrew Parkinson. **Dreamstime** 5(cr)
Musat; 11(t) Seread. **FLPA** 10 Jurgen & Christine Sohns; 13(tr) Ariadne Van Zandbergen. **Fotolia** 9(panel, t) Irochka.
iStock 5(tr) MarieHolding; 12 ACS15. **Nature Picture Library** 4–5 Edwin Giesbers; 13(tl) Anup Shah; 15(t) Sandesh
Kadur; 18–19 Andy Rouse. **Shutterstock** Heading panel (rt) Chris Kruger; Joke panel (rt) Tropinina Olga; Learn a Word
panel (rt) donatas1205; Learn a Word cartoon (rt) Virinaflora; 1 Sergey Gorshkov/Minden Pictures/FLPA; 3(r) Eric Isselee;
5(br) FloridaStock; 6 Stu Porter; 7(t) Dennis Donohue, (b) Sean Nel; 8–9(bg) Petrov Stanislav; 8(panel, tl) Ambient Ideas, (br)
tachyglossus, (panel, tr) Anna Tsekhmister, (tr); 9(heading panel, tl) sharpner, (heading, b) Lyolya; 11(r) Boleslaw Kubica; 13(bl)
Andreas Doppelmayr; 14(l and r) Eric Isselée; 15(b) Krzysztof Wiktor; 16–17(bg) Lucy Baldwin; 16(c) andere andrea petrlik,
(panel, b) donatas1205; 17(bl) Memo Angeles, (panels, br) LittleRambo; 19(b) Matt Hart; 20 Chris Kruger; 21(t) Magnus Haese.

LIBRARY OF CONGRESS CATALOGING-IN-PUBLICATION DATA

De la Bédoyère, Camilla, author.
 The wild life of big cats / Camilla de la Bedoyere.
    pages cm. — (The wild side)
 Includes index.
ISBN 978-1-4777-5491-7 (pbk.)
ISBN 978-1-4777-5492-4 (6 pack)
ISBN 978-1-4777-5490-0 (library binding)
1. Felidae—Juvenile literature. I. Title.
 QL737.C23D394 2015
 599.75—dc23
                              2014027095

Manufactured in the United States of America

CPSIA Compliance Information: Batch #CW15WM: For Further Information contact Rosen Publishing, New York, New York at 1-800-237-9932

Contents

What are you? 4

What do you hunt? 6

 Activity time 8

Where do you live? 10

What are your babies called? 12

What do you look like? 14

Puzzle time 16

How fast can you run? 18

Why do you roar? 20

The Lion that Couldn't Roar 22

Glossary, Index, and Websites 24

I am a big cat!

I am a type of animal called a mammal. I have fur and warm blood. I am a carnivore, which means I eat other animals.

Long tail
....

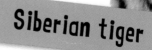

Siberian tiger

Q. What is a lion's favorite meal?

A. Baked beings on toast!

4

Lions, tigers, leopards, and cheetahs are all big cats.

Thick, soft fur

Whiskers

Paws with sharp claws

Small cats
Some wild cats are much smaller than big cats. Their size means they are fast and good at climbing.

Caracal

Ocelot

Lynx

How do you hunt?

Chasing

I chase other animals!

I use my big jaws and sharp claws to grab them. All big cats have strong senses. We can see, hear, and smell other animals from far away.

Q. What did the lion say to the gazelle?

A. Pleased to eat you!

Pouncing

Giant leap

Pumas have very strong back legs and can leap a long way. They sometimes pounce on their prey from above.

LEARN A WORD:
nocturnal
An animal that is awake at night and less active during the day.

Creeping

Night hunter

Most big cats are nocturnal. Lions, tigers, and leopards hunt at night. In the dark, they can creep up on other animals.

Activity time

Get ready to make and do!

Quiet as a cat

One person is Big Cat and faces a wall. The players must creep towards Big Cat. When Big Cat hears someone move he roars, and the players start again. To win, a player must reach Big Cat without being heard.

Draw me!

YOU WILL NEED: pencils · paper

1. Draw a wide oval for the body and a circle for the head.

2. Add two lines for the neck. Draw the legs and tail.

3. Draw two rounded ears. Add the nose, mouth and eyes.

Now color me in and give me a name!

8

Big cat card

Ask for help!

YOU WILL NEED:
8.5 x 11 inch card stock
scissors · glitter
colored pens and pencils

HERE'S HOW:
1. Fold the card in half and draw the outline of a tiger on one side. Make sure that both the head and tail reach the fold.

2. Cut out the tiger, leaving the folds at the head and tail.
3. Decorate your card.

Lion cupcakes

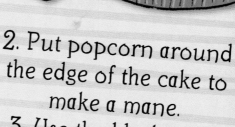

Ask for help!

YOU WILL NEED:
cupcakes · popcorn · knife
orange or yellow icing
black icing in a piping bag

HERE'S HOW:
1. Cover the top of each cake with orange or yellow icing and smooth it with the side of the knife.

2. Put popcorn around the edge of the cake to make a mane.
3. Use the black icing to draw the eyes, the nose, the mouth, and the whiskers.

9

Where do you live?

Sumatran tiger

I live
in the
hot jungle.

When it gets too hot I take
a cooling dip in the river.
There is lots of shade from
the trees where I can rest.

Cold and snow

Snow leopards have thick fur to keep them warm in their mountain home. They hunt sheep and hares.

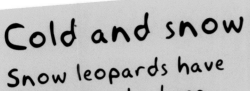

Q. What is striped and bouncy?

A. A tiger on a trampoline!

Tree cat

Leopards are good at climbing trees. They often hide their food in the branches. These big cats live in grasslands, forests, mountains, and deserts.

African leopard

11

What are your babies called?

My babies are called cubs!

3 months old

1

Newborn

Cubs are born blind and helpless. Their mother feeds them with milk.

2

Cubs rely on their mother for food and safety. She can move them quickly if they are in danger, by carrying them in her mouth.

Family life

Lions live in family groups called prides. Every lion in the pride helps to look after the cubs.

One year old

3 Cubs love to play-fight. It helps them learn to hunt, and makes them stronger as they grow up.

Q. What happened to the leopard who spent too long in the bath?

A. He was spotless!

What do you look like?

Black panther

Leopard

I am spotty.

All leopards have spots. Leopards or jaguars that have dark fur are known as black panthers. Their spots can still be seen.

Tiger

Q. What did the tiger say when he looked in the mirror?
A. Purr-fect!

Hard to spot

Tigers have stripy coats. This helps them to hide in long, dry grass and in the shadowy jungle.

Clouded wonder

This cat has cloud-shaped markings on its fur. Clouded leopards are shy cats, and very rare.

Puzzle time

Can you solve all the puzzles?

Jumble in the jungle

Can you unscramble these big cat names?

1. PARLEOD
2. ILON
3. GIRET
4. HEETCHA

Cheetah

ANSWERS: 1. Leopard 2. Lion 3. Tiger 4. Tiger

Clever cat

1. What is a lion family called – a pride or a pack?
2. Do leopards have spots or stripes?
3. Which cat runs fastest – the puma or the cheetah?

ANSWERS: 1. A pride 2. Spots 3. The cheetah

Whose cub?

Which cheetah parent has left Charlie the cub behind? Trace the path back to find out.

Charlie

Chelsea

Chester

Christina

ANSWER: Christina

Spot count

Count each leopard's spots. Who has the most, and who has the least?

Lawrence

Lisa

Leah

Odd one out

Can you find the odd one out in each box?

a
fang
tooth
tusk
jaws

b
stripe
fur
whisker
feather

c
fly   run
climb   jump

ANSWERS: a. Tusk b. Feather c. Fly

17

How fast can you run?

Cheetah

I am super speedy!

I can sprint faster than any other animal in the world, but only for short distances. My speed helps me when I am hunting.

Q. Which cat always wins at card games?
A. The cheetah!

LEARN A WORD:
swamp
A place with wet, boggy ground.

Super swimmer

Jaguars live near swamps and rivers. They are strong swimmers. They hunt animals such as turtles and alligators in water.

Why do you roar?

I roar to scare other animals.

My roar is so loud that other animals can hear me from far away. It warns them to keep out of my space.

Q. What happened when the lion ate the clown?

A. He felt funny!

Jaws and claws

Cheetahs have big jaws, long fangs and sharp claws! Their claws help them to grip the ground as they run.

LEARN A WORD:
fang
A long, pointed tooth is called a fang.

Cat fights

Big cats fight over food, mates, and space. They do not like to share!

21

The Lion that Couldn't Roar

The day that Stanley was born was a proud day for his family. He was a strong cub, with sharp claws and big teeth.

His mother and father said that he would be the leader of a pride, stronger than all other lions.

"Meow!" answered Stanley.

His mother and father looked at each other in horror. "Stanley can't roar!" they cried.

The next day, Stanley went to see Wise Buffalo in the forest. "Will I ever be able to roar?" he asked.

The Wise Buffalo looked thoughtful. At last he said, "You will never roar, unless you have faith in yourself."

"I have never heard of faith-in-yourself," said Stanley. "But I shall find it." He returned to the grassland and asked everyone where to look.

"Search underground," suggested Aardvark, poking his head out from his cool, dark burrow.

"Look in a book," said Baboon, who read a lot.

"It will be somewhere far away," said Giraffe, who gazed over the treetops.

So Stanley dug a hole in the dirt. He read Baboon's books and he climbed to the top of a tree and looked far away. Still, he could not roar.

That night, Stanley was so tired from looking for faith-in-yourself that he didn't notice he was sleeping with his head on a termite mound. As he slept, the furious termites emerged from their nest. The termite queen told all the bugs to climb over Stanley. Then she counted, "Three – two – one, go!", and all the termites bit Stanley as hard as they could with their little jaws.

"ROOOAAAAAAR!"

Stanley let out the loudest roar that had ever been heard on the grassland. It even woke up Wise Buffalo. "Sounds like Stanley had faith in himself after all!" he said.

By Camilla de la Bédoyère

Glossary

carnivore an animal that eats meat

creeping moving slowly, carefully, and sometimes quietly

jungle land overgrown with dense forest and tangled plant life

mammal a warm-blooded animal that has a backbone and hair, breathes air, and feeds milk to its young

mane long hair on the neck of a horse, lion, or other animal.

pride a group of lions

spotless has no spots; very clean

termite a small insect that eats wood

whisker a long hair growing near the mouth of some mammals, such as cats

Websites

For web resources related to the subject of this book, go to: **www.windmillbooks.com/weblinks** and select this book's title.

Index

carnivore 4

cheetah 5-6, 16, 18, 21

creeping 7

fang 17, 21

jungle 10, 15-16

leopard 5, 7, 11, 13-17

lion 4-7, 9, 12-13, 16-17 20, 22

mammal 4

mane 9

milk 12

nocturnal 7

pride 13, 16, 22

small cats 5

spotless 13

swamp 19

termite 23

tiger 4-5, 7, 9-11, 15-16

whisker 5, 9, 17